Coy Loves Cows

By Ellie Reid Rookes

For my favorite little

cattleman.

Always be yourself, Coy.

Auntie Ellie

There are many animals on the farm,

but Coy loves cows.

Pigs are smart, and eat our leftovers,

but Coy loves cows.

Cats cuddle us, and keep mice away,

but Coy loves cows.

Goats give us milk, and clean up the yard, but Coy loves cows.

Sheep make warm mittens,
and cute baby lambs,
but Coy loves cows.

Chickens make nuggets, and eggs to sell,
but Coy loves cows.

Donkeys can keep the pastures safe,
but Coy loves cows.

Horses can take you for a ride,

but Coy loves cows.

Dogs walk with us, and bark at strange cars, but Coy loves cows.

Roosters are... just the actual worst.

Coy loves cows.

There are many animals on the farm,
but Coy loves cows.

Ellie Reid Rookes is a school librarian and substitute teacher in small-town Saskatchewan, where she lives with her husband and two children.

She is inspired by her loved ones and the world around her.

This is her first publication.

Manufactured by Amazon.ca
Acheson, AB

12436230R00019